Visions of Football

Visions of Football

A CELEBRATION OF

THE WORLD'S FINEST FOOTBALL PHOTOGRAPHY

BY THE ALLSPORT PHOTOGRAPHIC AGENCY

ANDRE
DEUTSCH

First published in 1997 by
André Deutsch Ltd
106 Great Russell Street
London WC1B 3LJ

www.vci.co.uk

A CIP catalogue record for this book
is available from the British Library

ISBN 0 233 99177 8

Editor: Graham McColl
Editorial Contributors: Johan Cruyff and Alan Hansen
Project Director: James Nicholls

Designer and Picture Editor: Robert Kelland

Picture Editor: Tony Graham
Picture Research: Marc Glanville and Mark Trowbridge

Printed in Italy by Officine Grafiche DeAgostini

Alan Hansen's fee for his contribution to this book
has been donated to Southport Hospice and Southport Spinal Injury

Johan Cruyff's fee for his contribution to this book
has been donated to the Johan Cruyff Welfare Foundation

Brazilian World Cup victory, Los Angeles, 1994 (half-title page)
PHOTOGRAPH BY MIKE HEWITT

Diego Maradona (Argentina), World Cup, Mexico, 1986 (frontispiece)
PHOTOGRAPH BY DAVID CANNON

Nestor Sensini (Parma), Serie A, 1997 (title page)
PHOTOGRAPH BY CLAUDIO VILLA

Nery Pumpido (Argentina), World Cup, Italy, 1990 (left)
PHOTOGRAPH BY GERARD VANDYSTADT

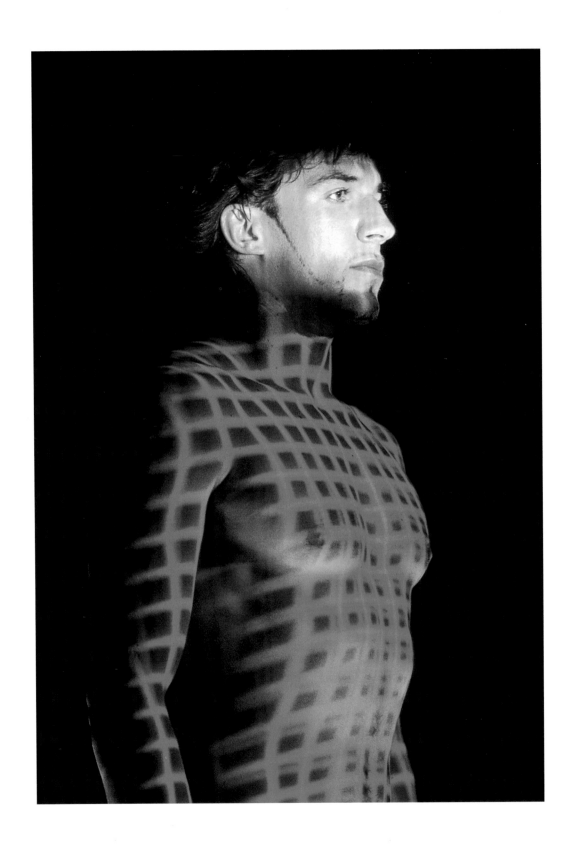

Alessandro Del Piero (Juventus), 1997

PHOTOGRAPH BY CLIVE MASON

foreword

by Keith Cooper
FIFA Director of Communications

When Pele entitled his autobiography *The Beautiful Game*, he was right – but not particularly original. For football has always been 'the beautiful game'. Sometimes, maybe its dynamic pace and the aggression it inevitably generates threaten to bely the description, but invariably these elements, too, only serve finally to enhance the game's visual image, adding new dimensions to its appeal.

In a world – and especially one of sport and of football in particular – that is becoming increasingly dazzled by the glare of the television spotlight, it is more important than ever to remember the contribution that still photography has played in the promotion of the beautiful game.

More than anyone else, the photographer must understand the game and the idiosyncrasies of its exponents in order to be sure to capture them in pictures that reveal what pages of words or hours of moving images cannot. Unlike the reporter or the commentator, the photographer has no second chance, no outside help, no instant playback to get his shot.

This kind of professional brinkmanship demands a level of concentration which translates into great pictures. And of course modern camera technology enhances the finished product, especially when in the hands of accomplished professionals.

FIFA is very aware of the debt that it owes the world's leading photographers and seeks to give them every reasonable opportunity to continue to supplement the world's football picture library. This book contains many prime examples of that library, from the extensive resources of Allsport, with the support of one of FIFA's most loyal sponsors, Canon.

I am sure that everyone browsing through this book will discover, probably not for the first time, just how beautiful our game truly is.

Leonardo (Paris St Germain) and Steve Harkness (Liverpool), Parc des Princes, 1997
PHOTOGRAPH BY SHAUN BOTTERILL

Olympic Stadium, Munich, Champions' League final, 1997

PHOTOGRAPH BY SHAUN BOTTERILL

introduction

by Allsport Photographic

The swift skills and fluidity of football make it the best-loved of the world's sports. In the 90 minutes of a match many tiny details of intensive effort are combined at high speed. There is so much happening so quickly that there is rarely time to stop and take stock. It is those qualities that make football enormously photogenic – when one of those moments of taut competition is frozen on film the effect is stunning.

These visions of football take cameos of motion that would have been part of a blur of action and preserve them for close, leisurely examination. Some pictures will provide vivid memories of a specific footballing time, place or occasion. Others will allow the viewer's imagination to supply a surrounding story. The majority of these images provide the perfect composite picture of the game of football as it stands on the verge of the 21st century. Other carefully-chosen pictorial gems acknowledge the game's illustrious past.

Supplementing the pictures are many words of wisdom on the nature of football from those who have experienced the game at the highest level and who have played unique roles in its progress. The special contributions from Johan Cruyff and Alan Hansen get under the skin of the game. Quotations from some of football's most talented players show how deeply the best players think about the game and their contributions to it.

Visions of Football takes an analytical look at the game, from the footballer's point of view of before, during and after a match. It begins with an examination of the tensions and anticipation preceding the kick-off, captures the split-second vitality of the action itself and concludes with the aftermath of the match and the beginning of the cycle back towards the next 90 minutes.

This book captures the essence of football: the poise and balance of the game's most accomplished players; the biting tackles; the colour of the fans; the excitement of the game's great occasions; and the glorious celebrations that make all the bruising work and excruciating application worthwhile.

In the 1990s, surrounding issues sometimes appear to be engulfing football. The pictures in this book provide a reminder of the basic beauties of the game that the people of the world have taken to their hearts.

Nigel Pearson (Sheffield Wednesday) and Mark Hughes (Manchester United), League Cup final, Wembley, 1991
PHOTOGRAPH BY SHAUN BOTTERILL

waiting for the whistle

Paul Ince (Internazionale), Milan, 1996 (above)
PHOTOGRAPH BY CLIVE BRUNSKILL

Boot lockers, Wolverhampton Wanderers, 1952 (right)
PHOTOGRAPH ALLSPORT HISTORICAL COLLECTION © HULTON GETTY

FA Cup final, Wembley, 1923
("waiting for the whistle", pages 10-11)
PHOTOGRAPH ALLSPORT HISTORICAL COLLECTION © HULTON GETTY

'**W**hen I went to Liverpool at first, if the game was at home we used to always go away on a Friday night but from 1982 on we would meet at about half past eleven on the Saturday morning and go for lunch at a hotel. Over the years I tended to eat less and less until I eventually had just a cup of tea because I'd feel better at three o'clock with nothing in my stomach. After our lunch we'd watch football on TV or read the papers.

'We'd arrive at the ground at about ten to two and the manager would tell you what the team was. Then you would go and leave your match-tickets for your guests before going back into the dressing-room. Between 2.15 and seven minutes to three, when you leave the dressing-room, was the worst time for tension, it was sheer purgatory. People would have different routines; I would do very little. Some people would go on to the pitch for a run to stretch their legs; I used to go and have a couple of runs, but not to stretch my legs, just to give me something to do.'

– ALAN HANSEN –

Bobby Robson (Barcelona coach),
Barcelona, 1996 (above)
PHOTOGRAPH BY BEN RADFORD

Zambian national team training,
Zambia, 1993 (right)
PHOTOGRAPH BY SIMON BRUTY

Street football, Zambia, 1993 (top)

Street football, Liverpool, 1996 (above)

Street football, Belfast, 1993 (right)

'he preparation would be different for an FA Cup final as it is probably different from any other game you ever play in because of the build-up. Obviously a European Cup final is the bigger game but, on the day, the FA Cup final has an atmosphere of its own, maybe because of the history attached to it and the build-up, which begins the minute the last League game has been played and then lasts for six or seven days. My first FA Cup final was in 1986 against Everton and the tension was so great I felt my legs had gone at the start of the game. I was 30 so I was able to fudge it and get through the game on experience but it must be quite an ordeal for a young player who has to cope with the occasion and who can't draw on his previous experience to get him through.'

– ALAN HANSEN –

Pele, training in England, 1963 (above)
PHOTOGRAPH ALLSPORT HISTORICAL COLLECTION © HULTON GETTY

World Cup, Mexico, 1986 (right)
PHOTOGRAPH BY BILLY STICKLAND

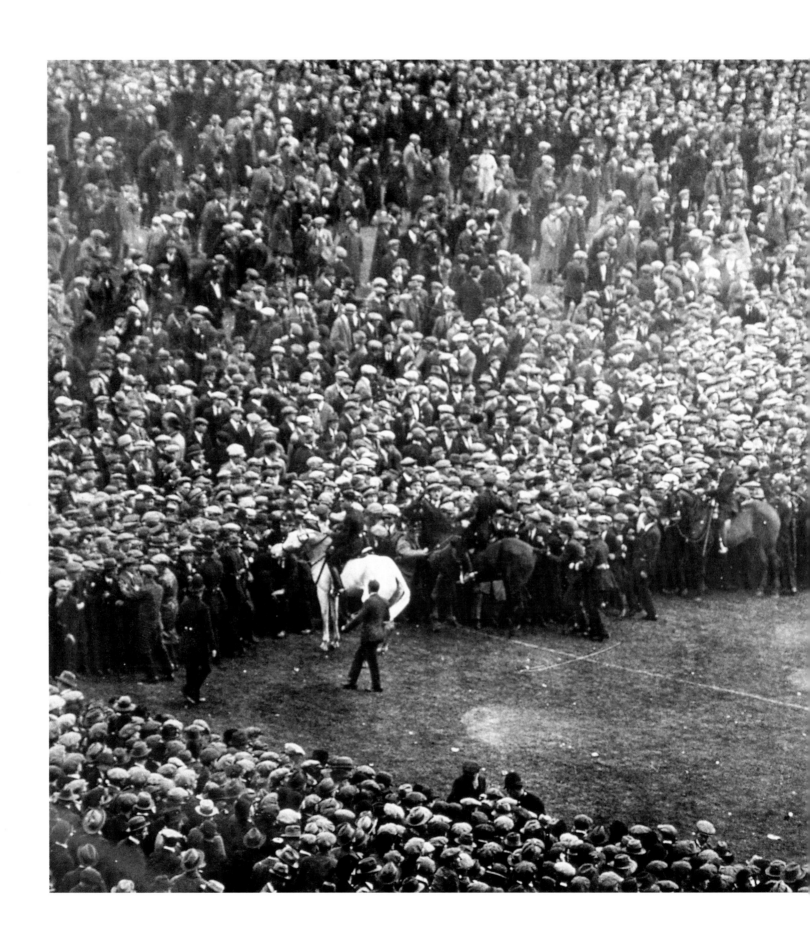

'In the dressing-room, before a match, I would leave the players alone. Everyone has their own way of preparing for the game. It would never pop into my mind to disturb that process. My last talk would therefore never last longer than 20 seconds. And even then I often had the idea that most players didn't hear what I said anyway.'

– JOHAN CRUYFF –

West Ham fans, Wembley, 1923 (top)

FA Cup final, West Ham v Bolton, Wembley, 1923 (left)

Programme seller, Goodison Park, 1986 (above)

Newcastle fans, Wembley, 1996 (above left)
PHOTOGRAPH BY MIKE HEWITT

Paris St Germain fans, Parc des Princes, 1997, (left)
PHOTOGRAPH BY STEPHANE KEMERAIRE

Italy fans, World Cup, Italy, 1990, (above)
PHOTOGRAPH BY SIMON BRUTY

Lens fans, UEFA Cup, Lens v Rome,
Parc des Princes, 1996 (above right)
PHOTOGRAPH BY VANDYSTADT

Fulham fans, FA Cup sixth round,
Fulham v Manchester United,
Craven Cottage, 1926 (right)
PHOTOGRAPH ALLSPORT HISTORICAL COLLECTION
© HULTON GETTY

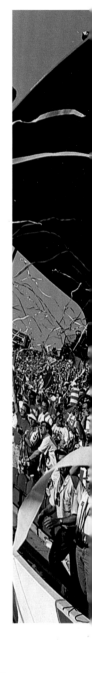

England v Argentina,
World Cup, Mexico,
1986 (left)

PHOTOGRAPH BY MICHAEL KING

Hillsborough,
European Championships,
1996 (above)

PHOTOGRAPH BY SIMON BRUTY

'at about twenty to three the manager would say a few words. He might have five minutes or 30 seconds depending on how we had been playing in the previous games. On the roof of the tunnel that leads on to the pitch at Anfield there is a sign that says "This Is Anfield". I always touched that sign on my way out on to the pitch. When you got out of the tunnel the nerves would disappear. It was like you had gone into some sort of room where someone said, "You won't be nervous again."

'At Partick Thistle you felt tension if you were going to play Celtic or Rangers but at Liverpool you could multiply that tension by any number you want – the expectation was that much greater. As my career at Liverpool progressed, things did not get easier on the nerves, because of the expectancy. Because Liverpool kept winning trophies people were expecting you to win games automatically. Then once you got past 30, you were put under a different kind of pressure with people saying that you were no longer good enough or that you were finished.'

– ALAN HANSEN –

Irish fans at Tolka Park, World Cup, USA, 1994 (top)

PHOTOGRAPH BY LORRAIN O'SULLIVAN

World Cup, USA, 1994 (above)

PHOTOGRAPH BY BILLY STICKLAND

Germany v Columbia, World Cup, Italy, 1990 (left)

PHOTOGRAPH BY DAVID CANNON

'Y ou can't get any higher
than the World Cup. It's
the biggest thing you'll play in.
It's as big a competition as you
can get in sport.

'In the World Cup in 1982
the Scots made a basic mistake of
travelling on that road along the
southern coast of Spain that
everybody hates. Your preparation
is everything and if your preparation is wrong then you're giving
yourself a big disadvantage even
before you set foot on the pitch.

'We were based in Soto-
grande and that was a big mistake. We played two of our games
in Malaga and that meant we had
to travel along that coast road,
which twists and turns all the
way, for 70 miles in 100 degrees
of heat. I don't think I've ever
travelled along that road without
being sick. Everybody hated that
road. So we were at an immediate
disadvantage even before our
matches began.

'Preparation is everything. If
you don't prepare properly you
diminish your chances.'

– ALAN HANSEN –

**Diego Maradona (Argentina),
World Cup, Italy, 1990**
PHOTOGRAPH BY SIMON BRUTY

across the white line

Joe Smith (Bolton) and G Kay (West Ham), FA Cup final, Wembley, 1923 (above)

PHOTOGRAPH ALLSPORT HISTORICAL COLLECTION © HULTON GETTY

Liverpool fans, FA Cup final, Wembley, 1992 (left)

PHOTOGRAPH BY DAVID CANNON

Liverpool fan, Anfield, 1992
("across the white line", pages 30-31)

PHOTOGRAPH BY ANTON WANT

West Ham fans, FA Cup final,
West Ham v Bolton, Wembley 1923 (above)

FA Cup fifth round, Swindon, 1928 (above left)

PHOTOGRAPHS ALLSPORT HISTORICAL COLLECTION © HULTON GETTY

Anderlecht v AC Milan, Champions' League, 1993 (left)

PHOTOGRAPH BY CLIVE BRUNSKILL

Mick McCarthy, Manager, Eire,
Eire v Russia, Dublin, 1996 (below)

PHOTOGRAPH BY BILLY STICKLAND

Gary Lineker (England) v Paraguay,
World Cup, Mexico, 1986 (right)

PHOTOGRAPH BY DAVID CANNON

'you wait for the first kick of the ball and look for it to give you confidence. Before you go out on the pitch you'll think back to the last five or six games and depending on whether you have been playing well or badly that will have an effect on your game. With your first pass or header you don't want to make a mistake or be edgy.

The first 20 minutes are always crucial. You want everybody in your team to be settling in well and looking comfortable.

'In the European Cup, all of the continental teams would play in the same manner. They would sit back and play the game very cagily. But in the English League, you never knew what to expect. Some teams would go hell-for-leather from the first minute. We used to love it if teams would go crazy in the first-half because the manager would say, "They'll never last at that pace." Because we were such a good passing team and liked to get it down and play, we would maintain a regular rhythm throughout the match and would still have a lot left to offer by the time they were a spent force.'

– ALAN HANSEN –

John Barnes (Liverpool) and Andy Gray (Crystal Palace), Selhurst Park, 1990 (left)
PHOTOGRAPH BY DAN SMITH

Jan Suchoparek (Czech Republic) and Fredi Bobic (Germany), European Championships, Old Trafford, 1996, (right)
PHOTOGRAPH BY SIMON BRUTY

Edgar Davids (AC Milan)
and Mario Melchiot (Ajax),
Amsterdam Arena, 1996 (left)

PHOTOGRAPH BY SHAUN BOTTERILL

Ed Pustavitch (Dallas Burn)
and Roberto Donadoni
(New York Metrostars),
Major League Soccer,
USA, 1996 (right)

PHOTOGRAPH BY ANDY LYONS

Stanley Matthews, RAF, 1943 (above)

PHOTOGRAPH ALLSPORT HISTORICAL COLLECTION © HULTON GETTY

Ajax v Juventus, European Cup final, Rome, 1996 (right)

PHOTOGRAPH BY SHAUN BOTTERILL

Ruud Gullit (Holland) and Rudi Voeller (West Germany), European Championships, West Germany, 1988

Photograph by David Cannon

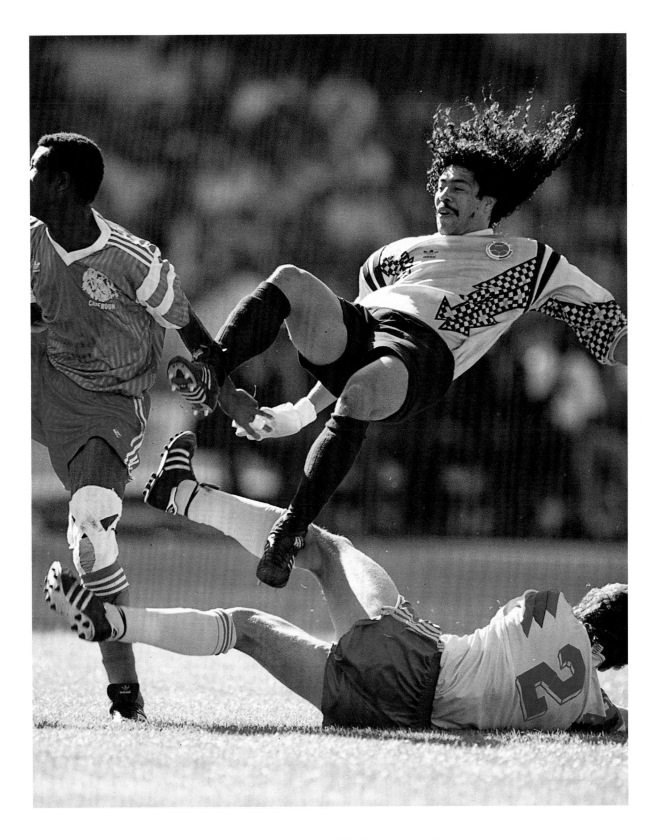

Rene Higuita (Columbia), World Cup, Italy, 1990

PHOTOGRAPH BY DAVID CANNON

'Concentration is enormously important and the more you play the more you learn what to expect of yourself. You learn to concentrate even when the ball is well away from you. If you lose concentration you are history as a defender but it is even worse for a goalkeeper. He just has to lose concentration once and he is likely to have lost a goal.

'As a defender you impose yourself on your direct opponent by staying tight on him and not giving him any joy. You make sure you are tight on him and don't give him time and space. You make sure that if he is going to get anything against you then he will really have had to do something special.

'A captain is the manager's voice on the pitch. If the manager has any instructions he will give them to the captain and the captain then has the responsibility of putting them into action. A captain must be vocal sometimes but, most importantly, he has to lead by example, especially for the younger players.'

– ALAN HANSEN –

Marco Van Basten and
Frank Rijkaard (Holland),
and Karl-Heinz Riedle
(West Germany),
European Championships
1996 (above)

PHOTOGRAPH BY SIMON BRUTY

Alex McLeish (Scotland),
John Fashanu, Stuart Pearce
and Des Walker (England),
Hampden Park, 1989 (left)

PHOTOGRAPH BY DAVID CANNON

Claudio Cannigia
and Oscar Ruggeri (Argentina)
and Walter Zenga and
Paolo Maldini (Italy),
World Cup, Italy, 1990 (right)

PHOTOGRAPH BY SIMON BRUTY

Keith Houchen (Coventry), FA Cup final, Wembley, 1987 (above and right)

PHOTOGRAPHS BY DAVID CANNON

John Lukic (Leeds) v PSV Eindhoven, UEFA Cup, Philips SV Stadion, 1995 (above left)

PHOTOGRAPH BY BEN RADFORD

Walter Zenga (Inter Milan) v Norwich, UEFA Cup, San Siro, 1994 (above right)

PHOTOGRAPH BY CLIVE BRUNSKILL

Danish celebration, European Championships final, Sweden, 1992 (right)

PHOTOGRAPH BY SHAUN BOTTERILL

I don't ever set targets. I just do my job and ask the same of other people. I never shoot my mouth off. I just go out and do the work.

Paolo Montero (Juventus), Stadio del Alpi, 1996 (above)
PHOTOGRAPH BY CLAUDIO VILLA

Les Ferdinand (Newcastle), St James' Park, 1995 (left)
PHOTOGRAPH BY MARK THOMPSON

Paul Gascoigne and Darren Anderton (England),
European Championships, Wembley, 1996 (above)

Darren Anderton and Alan Shearer (England),
European Championships, Wembley, 1996 (right)

PHOTOGRAPHS BY SHAUN BOTTERILL

❛I want to win and I want to win badly.
It is the way I have been brought up
and the only way I know. If that is a fault
then I wish there were more who shared my attitude.
I don't need to look at newspapers to know
if I have played well. I don't need other people
to tell me. Goals don't equal good performances –
all they can do, if anything, is cover up
for bad ones, which is wrong.❜

– ALAN SHEARER –
NEWCASTLE UNITED AND ENGLAND

Jan Aage Fjortoft (Middlesbrough) and Tim Flowers (Blackburn),
Riverside Stadium, Middlesbrough, 1995 (left)

PHOTOGRAPH BY CLIVE BRUNSKILL

Kubilay Turkyilmaz (Switzerland) and Colin Calderwood (Scotland),
European Championships, Villa Park, 1996 (above left)

PHOTOGRAPH BY SIMON BRUTY

Robbie Fowler (Liverpool) and Roy Keane (Manchester United),
FA Cup final, Wembley, 1996 (centre)

Sergi Barjuan (Barcelona) and George Weah (Paris St Germain),
European Cup, Paris, 1995 (above right)

PHOTOGRAPHS BY SHAUN BOTTERILL

'I often hear that managers have problems with communicating their ideas to their players during a match. But I was never really bothered by it. If I wanted to get a message through, I mostly gave the information to a player who was standing close to the bench. He would then deliver the order to the person whom it was meant for.'

– JOHAN CRUYFF –

Carlos Trucco (Bolivia) and
Jurgen Klinsmann (Germany),
World Cup, USA, 1994 (right)

Marcio Santos (Brazil) and
Karl-Heinz Riedle (Germany),
US Cup, Washington, 1993
(opposite)

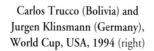

PHOTOGRAPHS BY SHAUN BOTTERILL

Hugo Sanchez (Mexico) booked by referee George Courtney,
World Cup, Mexico, 1986 (above)

PHOTOGRAPH BY DAVID CANNON

Roberto Donadoni (AC Milan) fouled by Nestor Sensini (Parma),
Stadio Tardini, Parma, 1993 (left)

PHOTOGRAPH BY CLIVE BRUNSKILL

Francois Dolmoe (Cameroon)
and Pierre Mel (Ivory Coast),
African Nations Cup,
Ivory Coast, 1984 (left)

PHOTOGRAPH BY DAVID CANNON

Torben Piechnik (Liverpool),
Anfield, 1992 (below)

PHOTOGRAPH BY MIKE HEWITT

David Busst (Coventry City) breaks his leg, Old Trafford, 1996

PHOTOGRAPH BY SHAUN BOTTERILL

'When any of the three Liverpool managers that I played under – Joe Fagan, Kenny Dalglish and Bob Paisley – spoke, 90 per cent of the time they were near the mark although the way it was put over was different. And if someone is 90 per cent right most of the time then you are always going to listen to them. Joe Fagan wasn't as forceful as the other two but he was so respected in the dressing-room he didn't need to say things forcefully. If Joe Fagan said something to me then I would always listen.'

– ALAN HANSEN –

Kenny Dalglish (Liverpool manager),
FA Cup final v Everton, Wembley, 1989 (left)
PHOTOGRAPH BY SIMON BRUTY

Liverpool fans, Charity Shield, Wembley, 1986 (above)
PHOTOGRAPH BY DAVID CANNON

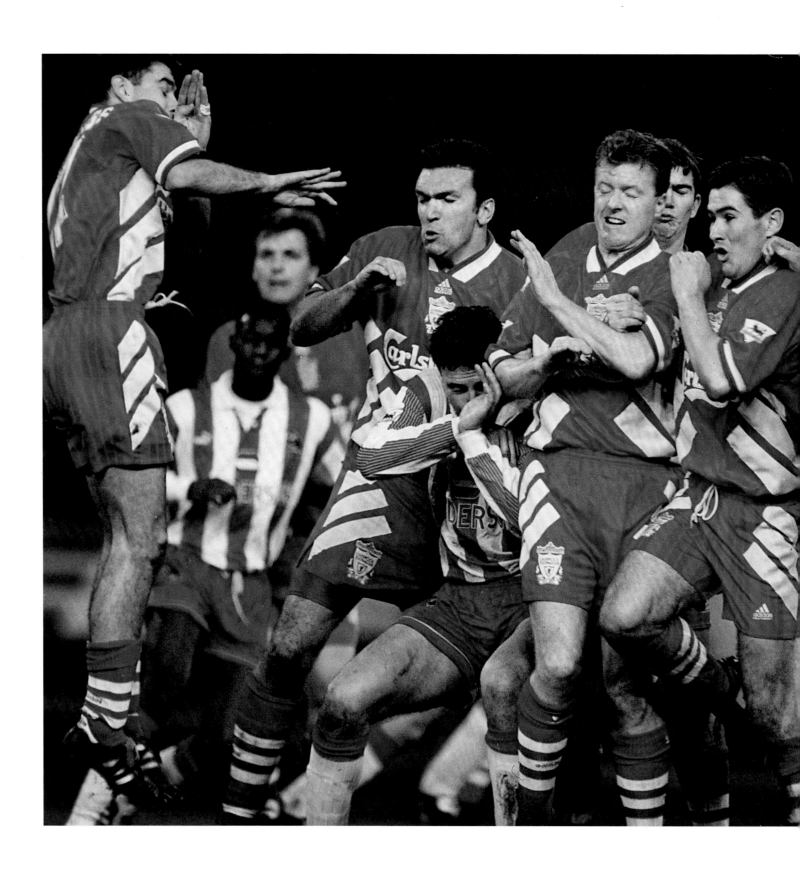

David Ginola (Newcastle), St James' Park, 1996 (above)

PHOTOGRAPH BY MARK THOMSON

Liverpool defensive wall, Hillsborough, 1993 (left)

PHOTOGRAPH BY ANTON WANT

Giants' Stadium, New York, World Cup, 1994 (above)
PHOTOGRAPH BY SIMON BRUTY

Guiseppe Bergomi (Italy) and Emil Kostadinov (Bulgaria),
World Cup, Azteca Stadium, Mexico, 1986 (right)
PHOTOGRAPH BY MICHAEL KING

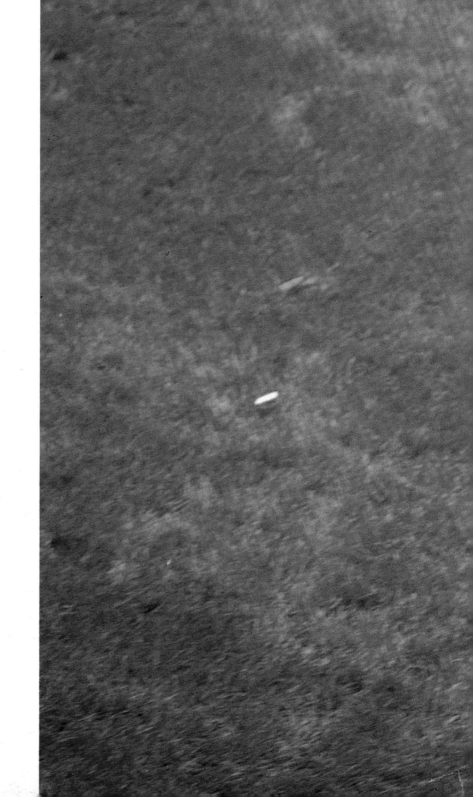

‘Putting the ball into the net is ultimately the most important thing.’

– MICHEL PLATINI –
JUVENTUS AND FRANCE

Rivelino (Brazil), World Cup final, Mexico, 1970 (above)

PHOTOGRAPH ALLSPORT HISTORICAL COLLECTION © HULTON GETTY

Tibor Selymes (Romania), European Championships, Newcastle, 1996 (right)

PHOTOGRAPH BY CLIVE BRUNSKILL

“Whatever anyone else says, no system is greater than the players
out on the pitch. You can play any style that you like,
the important thing is to create a strong group.”

– CESARE MALDINI –
MANAGER, ITALY

Steve Bruce (Manchester United), Elland Road, 1996 (left)
PHOTOGRAPH BY CLIVE BRUNSKILL

Ryan Giggs, London, 1996 (above)
PHOTOGRAPH BY CLIVE MASON

Steve Bruce (Manchester United)
and Ian Rush (Liverpool),
Old Trafford, 1995 (above)

PHOTOGRAPH BY SHAUN BOTTERILL

Ryan Giggs (Manchester United),
Dominic Matteo, Jason McAteer and Michael
Thomas (Liverpool), Old Trafford, 1996 (right)

PHOTOGRAPH BY CLIVE BRUNSKILL

I did have this quality of being able to sway around players like a matador. That was due to my great sense of balance. It is the most important quality if you want to be able to ride challenges. If that bull is rushing at you at 100 miles an hour and you've got to get out of the way, you need balance. I had perfect balance from an early age.

I never had to think about the angle that a player was coming in at me; I simply used to adjust myself.

It takes a sort of bravery as well, to take on people when you know they will try and clobber you.

– GEORGE BEST –
MANCHESTER UNITED AND NORTHERN
IRELAND

George Best (Manchester United) and Ron Harris (Chelsea), Old Trafford, 1968 (left)

Gordon Banks (England), training at Roehampton, 1969 (right)

'We played in the European Cup final in 1981 against Real Madrid, who had won that trophy a few times, at the Parc des Princes in Paris. Before the game I went out on to the pitch and where the Real Madrid fans were they had a massive banner that was the biggest banner I have ever seen in my life – it stretched the whole length of the ground. It really gave you a sense of the occasion and of the size of the club that we were up against.

'During a match you would never hear the fans unless you were having a hard time in front of your own fans. Then you would feel that they were a bit edgy or jumpy.

'Unless the support is tremendously vocal you don't notice them at all. In Europe the first 20 minutes is important because you want to keep the crowd quiet. If you are playing away in Europe it puts a bit more pressure on you if the crowd is fully behind them.'

– ALAN HANSEN –

**Scottish FA Cup final, Celtic v Dundee United,
Hampden Park, 1988**

PHOTOGRAPH BY DAVID CANNON

At Borussia Dortmund, everything is done at speed. You eventually get used to it. You have to – otherwise you don't survive. It's sink or swim but being here has improved my touch. I'm also learning more about the game. I sit in an anchor role and don't go charging forward the way I used to in Scotland. Everyone knows their function and they stick to it. Back home that kind of discipline is rare.

– PAUL LAMBERT –
BORUSSIA DORTMUND
AND SCOTLAND

Keith Mason (Witton) and Neil Masters (Colchester)
FA Trophy final, Wembley, 1992 (above)

Chris Armstrong (Tottenham Hotspur),
White Hart Lane, 1996 (right)

PHOTOGRAPHS BY GARY M PRIOR

Brian Kidd, George Graham,
Pat Crerand, Frank McLintock,
George Best and John Radford,
Manchester United v Arsenal,
Old Trafford, 1967

PHOTOGRAPH
ALLSPORT HISTORICAL COLLECTION
© HULTON GETTY

Raffaele Ametrano (Juventus)
and Paolo Maldini (AC Milan),
San Siro, 1996 (right)

Roberto Baggio (AC Milan),
San Siro, 1996 (opposite)

PHOTOGRAPHS BY CLAUDIO VILLA

‘The whole thing about the game is mastering the ball and controlling it.
That's what makes the Brazilians so good. If you get to know the ball you can judge its speed and the angle
at which it is coming to you. Then you can weight your pass to your team-mate just right. And the way to get that ability
is just by working with the ball all the time. If you work with the ball and develop perfect control then the rest comes.
People go on about one-touch stuff a lot nowadays. To me, that's a lot of rubbish. All the tactics in the world
are no good if a player can't take control of the ball when it comes to him.’

– JIMMY JOHNSTONE –
CELTIC AND SCOTLAND

Nicolas Anelka (Paris St Germain), Parc des Princes, 1996 (above)

PHOTOGRAPH BY CHRISTOPHE GUIAUDE

Fabrizio Ravanelli (Juventus), European Cup final, 1996 (right)

PHOTOGRAPH BY SHAUN BOTTERILL

Jorge Campos (LA Galaxy),
Major League Soccer,
USA, 1996 (left)

PHOTOGRAPH BY STEPHEN DUNN

Turkish fans, PSV v Galatasaray,
Parc des Princes, 1996 (right)

PHOTOGRAPH BY RICHARD MARTIN

Ian Wright, Paul Merson and
Patrick Vieira (Arsenal),
Selhurst Park, 1996 (below right)

PHOTOGRAPH BY MIKE HEWITT

Diego Maradona (Argentina),
World Cup, Italy, 1990 (above left)
PHOTOGRAPH BY BILLY STICKLAND

Diego Maradona (Argentina),
World Cup, Italy, 1990 (above centre)
PHOTOGRAPH BY BILLY STICKLAND

Diego Maradona (Napoli),
Italian Serie A, 1988 (above right)
PHOTOGRAPH BY DAVID CANNON

Diego Maradona (Argentina) v Belgium,
World Cup, Spain, 1982 (right)
PHOTOGRAPH BY STEVE POWELL

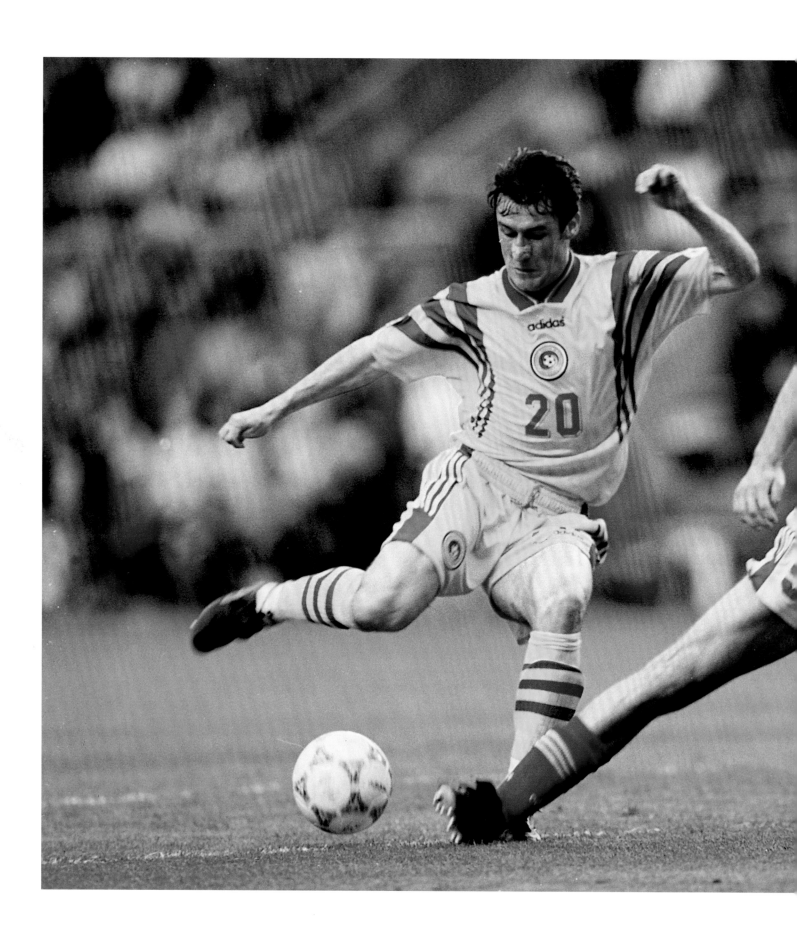

Antonio Benarrivo (Italy) and Sigurd Rushfeldt (Norway),
World Cup, USA, 1994 (above)

PHOTOGRAPH BY CHRIS COLE

Viovel Moldovan (Romania) and Laurent Blanc (France),
European Championships, Newcastle, 1996 (left)

PHOTOGRAPH BY CLIVE BRUNSKILL

half-time

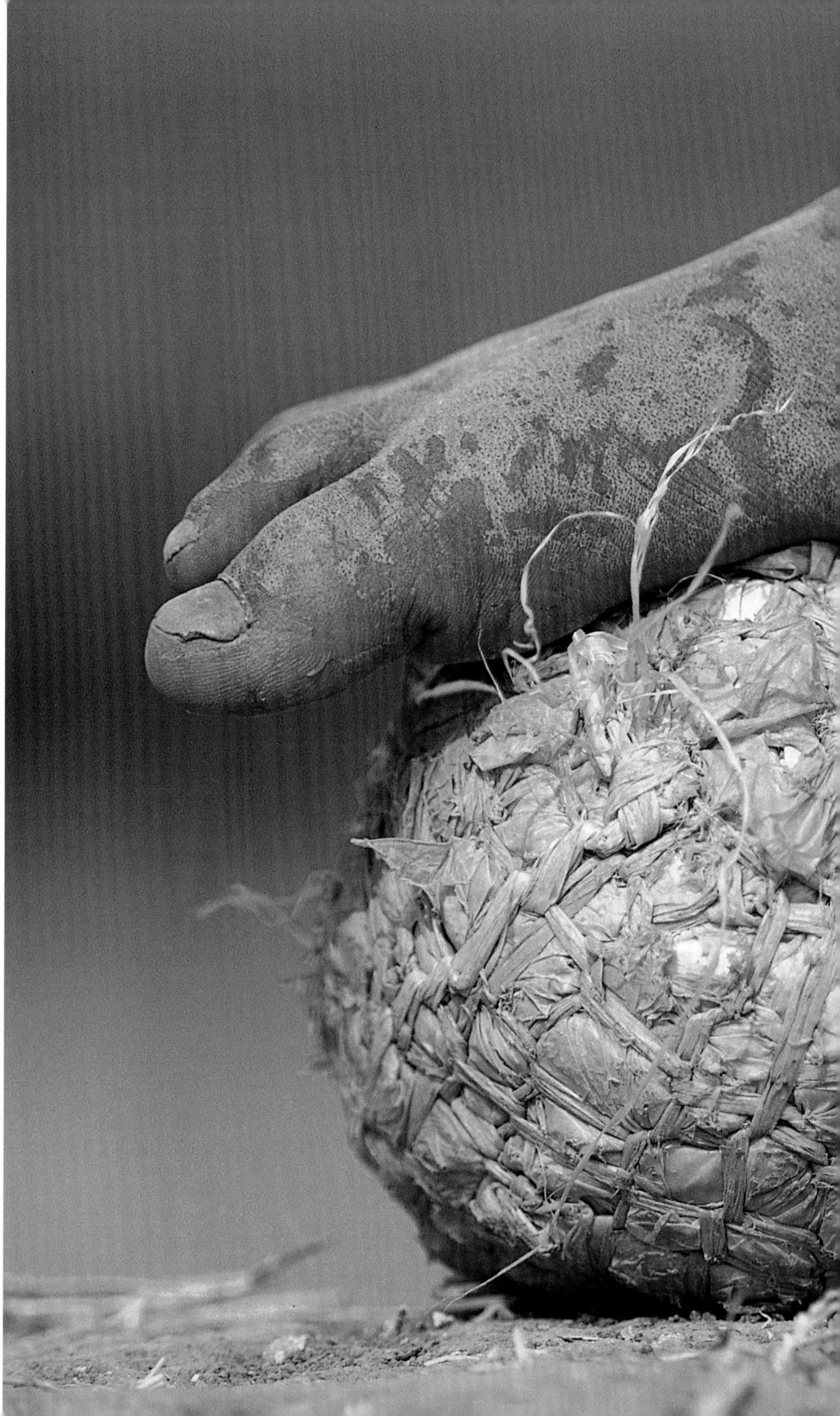

half-time

'half-time is the only possibility for a coach to do some work. Within 15 minutes you have to explain all your impressions of the match to the team. They would be based on the fact that football is a game of mistakes. So first I would tell my players what they had done wrong and how to try to minimalise those problems in the second half. Then I would put my finger on what our opponents were doing. Everything would be simple but very direct. As I said, you only have 15 minutes to get your ideas across to the players.'

– JOHAN CRUYFF –

Coventry dressing room, 1997 (above)
PHOTOGRAPH BY GRAHAM CHADWICK

Inter fans, Serie A, San Siro, Milan, 1989 (left)
PHOTOGRAPH BY DAVID CANNON

Children's football, Zambia, 1993
("half-time", pages 92-93)
PHOTOGRAPH BY SIMON BRUTY

George Best (Manchester United), 1965 (top)

Schoolboy football, 1935 (above)

Bobby Charlton (Manchester United), 1958 (right)

Scotland fans (right)

PHOTOGRAPH BY BEN RADFORD

Morocco fan (below)

PHOTOGRAPH BY CLIVE BRUNSKILL

Barcelona fans (below right)

PHOTOGRAPH BY SIMON BRUTY

Holland fan (above)

PHOTOGRAPH BY BEN RADFORD

Norway fan (left)

PHOTOGRAPH BY CHRIS COLE

Inter fans (right)

PHOTOGRAPH BY DAVID CANNON

'at half-time you could never predict what the manager was going to say to you unless you were something like 4-0 up or 2-0 down, although it was very rarely the case at Liverpool that we'd be losing like that. It would all depend on how the game was going. If a game was tight and you were playing well they'd say you were playing badly. If you were playing badly they'd say you were playing well. It was all psychological, and it was done to keep you on your toes. You never knew what to expect – and over the years it worked extremely well.

'The half-time interval can be a killer for teams – you can be so far on top you can become complacent or if a team is behind the breather can give them a chance to pick themselves up.

'You would have a cup of tea and a sit-down. Basically the manager would say a few words and then you just waited to get out and get on with it. I didn't like having a long half-time break, you really just want to get on with the game.'

– ALAN HANSEN –

African Cup of Nations, Johannesburg, 1996 (right)
PHOTOGRAPH BY GARY M PRIOR

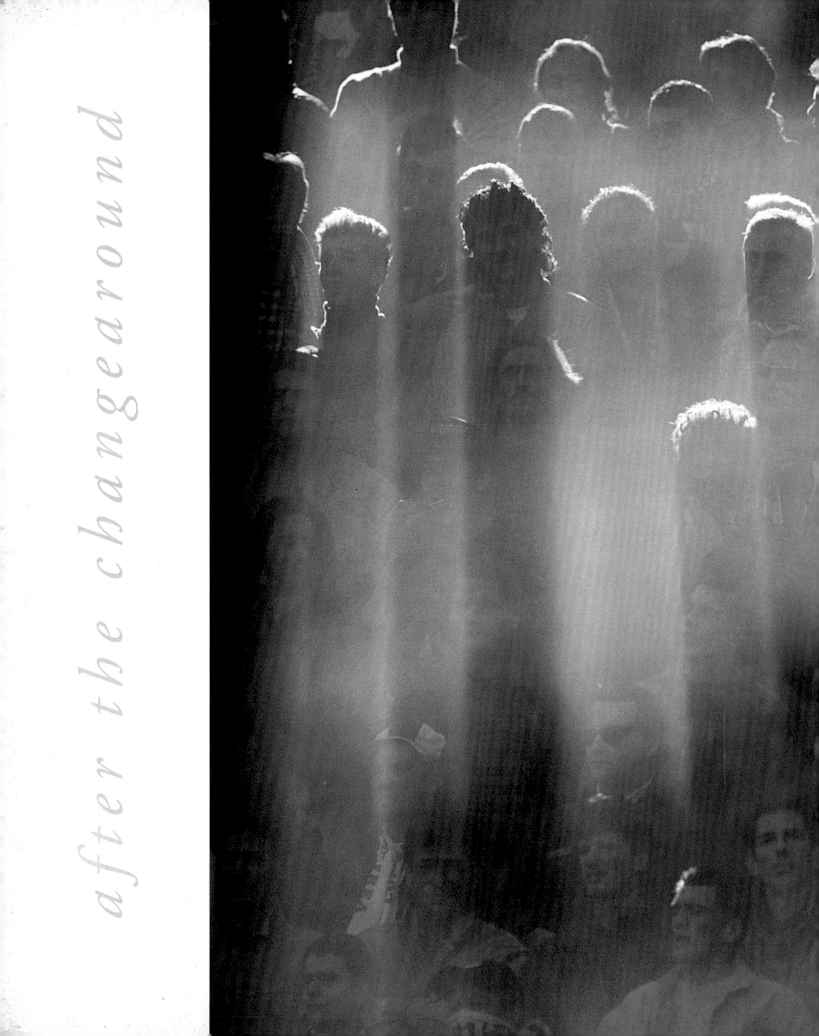

after the changearound

after the
changearound

Jury's Hotel, Dublin, World Cup, 1994 (right)
PHOTOGRAPH BY JAMES MEEHAN

Juventus fans, San Siro, 1992
("after the changearound", pages 102-103)
PHOTOGRAPH BY SIMON BRUTY

Columbian children,
Santa Cruz, 1997 (above left)
PHOTOGRAPH BY MARK THOMPSON

African children,
Ivory Coast, 1984 (below left)
PHOTOGRAPH BY DAVID CANNON

Bruce Grobbelaar (Liverpool),
St James' Park, 1993 (right)
PHOTOGRAPH BY SHAUN BOTTERILL

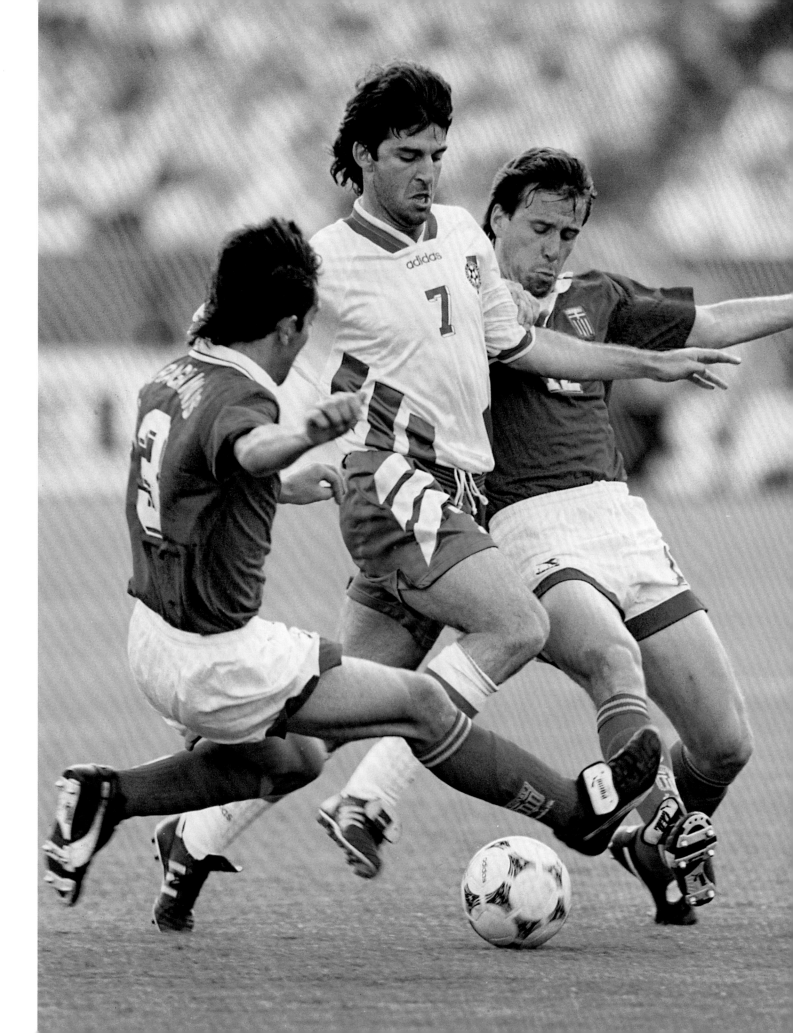

Guido Buchwald (West Germany) and Carlos Enrique Estrada (Columbia), World Cup, 1990 (above left)

PHOTOGRAPH BY DAVID CANNON

Dejan Savicevic (Milan) and Roger Mendy (Pescara), Serie A, Pescara, 1992 (above right)

PHOTOGRAPH BY BEN RADFORD

Emil Kostadinov (Bulgaria) and Vaios Karagiannis and Spiros Marangos (Greece), World Cup, 1994 (left)

PHOTOGRAPH BY JONATHON DANIEL

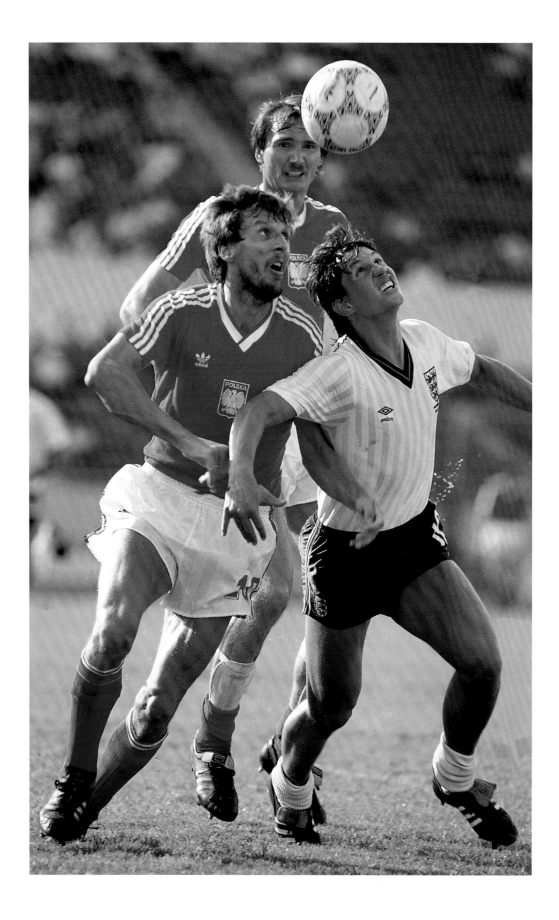

Stephan Majewski (Poland)
and Gary Lineker (England),
World Cup, Mexico,
1986 (left)

Photograph by David Cannon

Tiffany Roberts (USA),
Algarve Cup, USA v Norway,
Portugal, 1994 (right)

Photograph by Shaun Botterill

'I know I still have to work a lot on all the different aspects of my game.
For example, I tend to lose my nerve when I find myself alone in front of a goalkeeper.
I still lose too many of those duels.'

– THIERRY HENRY –
AS MONACO AND FRANCE

 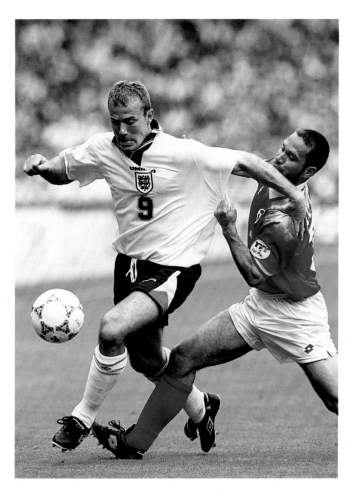

Michael Emenalo (Nigeria) and Gabriel Batistuta (Argentina), World Cup, USA, 1994 (left)

PHOTOGRAPH BY BEN RADFORD

Dennis Bergkamp (Holland) and Paul McGrath (Eire), World Cup, USA, 1994 (above left)

Alan Shearer (England) and Yves Quentin (Switzerland),
European Championships, Wembley, 1996 (above right)

PHOTOGRAPHS BY SHAUN BOTTERILL

Disabled people playing football, Norway, 1994 (above)

PHOTOGRAPH BY SHAUN BOTTERILL

Wagner de Souza (Santos) and Nidelson Silva (Toros Neza),
Mexican Championship, 1996 (left)

PHOTOGRAPH BY DAVID LEAH

Rasheed Yekeni (Nigeria),
World Cup, USA, 1994 (above)
PHOTOGRAPH BY GARY M PRIOR

David Seaman (Arsenal),
European Cup-Winners' Cup semi-final
v Sampdoria, Genoa, 1995 (right)
PHOTOGRAPH BY GARY M PRIOR

Francesco Totti (Roma),
Stadio Olimpico, 1994 (below)

PHOTOGRAPH BY SHAUN BOTTERILL

Brian Clough
(Nottingham Forest manager),
City Ground, 1993 (right)

PHOTOGRAPH BY DAVID CANNON

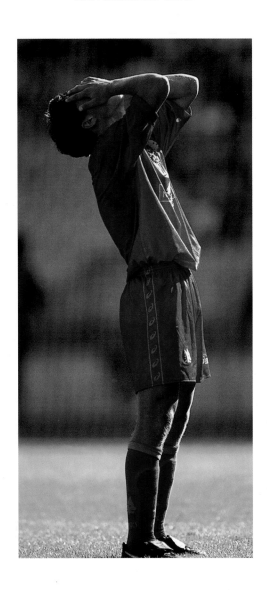

‘Individual speed is an advantage. But to run without purpose is of no value. It is the ball that must be moved about quickly, ideally on first contact. To run with it is too often only wasting valuable attacking time.’

– FERENC PUSKAS –
REAL MADRID AND HUNGARY

David Seaman (Arsenal), Highbury, 1997 (above)
PHOTOGRAPH BY BEN RADFORD

Bruce Grobbelaar (Liverpool), Old Trafford, 1985 (left)
PHOTOGRAPH BY MICHAEL KING

**Erik Thorstvedt (Tottenham Hotspur),
White Hart Lane, 1990** (right)
PHOTOGRAPH BY HOWARD BOYLAN

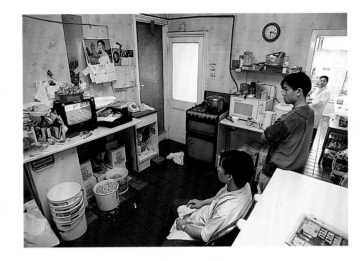

Geoff Hurst (England),
World Cup final,
Wembley, 1966 (left)

PHOTOGRAPH ALLSPORT HISTORICAL
COLLECTION © HULTON GETTY

Chinese take-away, Liverpool,
European Championships, 1996
(above right)

PHOTOGRAPH BY BEN RADFORD

Disallowed goal,
Bugaria v Romania,
European Championships,
St James' Park, 1996
(right)

PHOTOGRAPH BY STU FORSTER

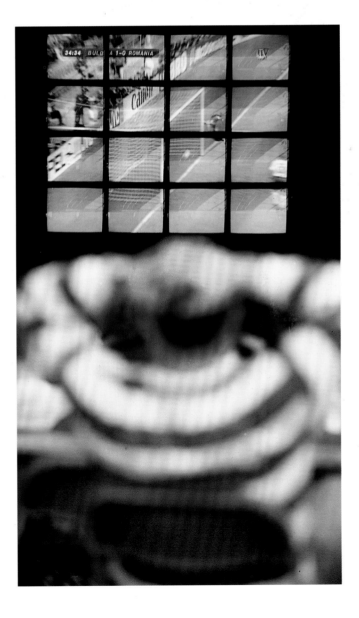

One spends one's time listening to, assessing one's body. The human body isn't made to play football. So you have to force it, gently, above all when age begins to weigh on you. I spend time talking with my body. The body never lies. I know that one day it will say, "Stop! I can no longer bear what you're asking me!" I cannot say whether that day is coming. The better I know my body, the more able I am to decide if it's demanding a massage or some training, some work, some effort, or a rest. Thanks to such attention, I am still capable of playing.

– RUUD GULLIT –
CHELSEA PLAYER-MANAGER

**West Germany v Argentina,
World Cup final, Mexico, 1986**

PHOTOGRAPH BY DAVID CANNON

Frank Rijkaard (Ajax),
European Cup final,
Vienna, 1995 (left)
PHOTOGRAPH BY CLIVE BRUNSKILL

Crystal Palace celebrate,
Highbury, 1994 (opposite left)
PHOTOGRAPH BY PHIL COLE

Arsenal celebrate,
FA Cup final, Wembley, 1993
(opposite centre)
PHOTOGRAPH BY SHAUN BOTTERILL

Cameroon celebrate,
World Cup, Italy, 1990
(opposite right)
PHOTOGRAPH BY BILLY STICKLAND

'If you are winning or playing well you really enjoy playing. I was never a great tackler but we had several very good tacklers in our side so the tackling would be done by them. I was a good header of the ball and scored a few goals with my head because if you're six foot two that's liable to happen. But I was never great in the air because I was not aggressive enough in challenging for the ball.

'But football is all about knowing your strengths and weaknesses and making the most of the ability that you do have. What I liked was getting the ball at my feet, giving it and getting it back and making runs out of defence. At all times I would try to get the ball at my feet and I was great at hitting it 30 or 40 yards into space. I really enjoyed doing that.

'The final ten minutes can be the most important of the match. Again it depends on how the match is going. If you are getting beaten you have to find ways of getting back into the game and doing something different. It's a vital time: if you score one or lose one it's difficult to come back from it.

'Physically, I think that if you were feeling good at the start of the game you would be feeling good at the end.'

– ALAN HANSEN –

'The more important the match, the more highly-charged the atmosphere. I have experienced a lot of important games. Finals! Fortunately I played in a lot of them.

'As a manager the most memorable match in my career

should be Barcelona's 1-0 victory over Sampdoria in the 1992 European Champions' Cup final at Wembley. That is from a prestigious point of view. It was the first time Barcelona had ever won that trophy. But from a managing point of view it is Ajax's 1-0 win over Lokomotiv Leipzig in the 1987 European Cup-Winners' Cup final.

'Before that game all the odds were against us. Important players were suspended and on the eve of the match I lost some other key players because of injuries. I was then forced to send a team on to the pitch that was the youngest that had ever played in the final of a European competition. To have such a group of teenagers believe that they could beat their much more experienced opponents requires maximum skill as a manager. The taste of victory afterwards is sweeter than ever.'

– JOHAN CRUYFF –

**Johan Cruyff,
World Cup final,
West Germany,
1974** (above)
PHOTOGRAPH
ALLSPORT HISTORICAL COLLECTION
© HULTON GETTY

**Brian McClair
(Manchester United)
and David Kelly
(Sunderland),
Roker Park, 1997** (right)
PHOTOGRAPH BY STU FORSTER

❝The French simply work at being fast. In the modern game now, at least the way the Europeans play it, you are nothing without speed. At Monaco we do sprint work all the time. I'm talking about trying to run while pulling weights behind you. I've also done hurdles and special work on my calves, ankles and thighs.

'They analyse your blood to see what you are lacking and they look at the muscles in your legs to see which ones tire the most and then they know what to work on improving. The French are physically sharper and when you add that to the work they put in on their technique, it's quite a combination.

'The skill level here is much better than in Britain. When I first came I couldn't tell in training which guys were the defenders because everyone seemed so comfortable on the ball.

'Here it's a slow, slow pace, keeping possession, tiring the opposition out then, when a gap emerges in the last third of the pitch, bang! Foreign teams seem better prepared to play the killer pass and finish it off.❞

– JOHN COLLINS –
AS MONACO AND SCOTLAND

Terry Butcher (England),
World Cup qualifier, Sweden, 1989 (above)
PHOTOGRAPH BY DAVID CANNON

Nicola Berti (Italy) and Paul Caliguri (USA),
World Cup, Italy, 1990 (left)
PHOTOGRAPH BY SIMON BRUTY

Diego Maradona (Argentina),
World Cup, Rome, 1990 (above)
PHOTOGRAPH BY BILLY STICKLAND

Graeme Souness
(Liverpool Manager),
Plough Lane, 1991 (right)
PHOTOGRAPH BY DAVID CANNON

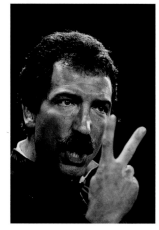

Mexico fan,
World Cup, Mexico, 1986 (left)
PHOTOGRAPH BY VANDYSTADT

Carlos Valderrama
(Tampa Bay Mutiny),
Major League soccer,
Rose Bowl, 1996 (above)

PHOTOGRAPH BY SIMON P BARNETT

Lee Sharpe
(Manchester United),
Old Trafford, 1996 (right)

PHOTOGRAPH BY SHAUN BOTTERILL

Pierluigi Collina (referee),
Serie A, Italy, 1993 (above)

PHOTOGRAPH BY CLIVE BRUNSKILL

Paul Gascoigne (Rangers)
Ibrox, 1995 (left)

PHOTOGRAPH BY PHIL COLE

Diego Maradona (Argentina),
World Cup, Mexico, 1986 (above)

PHOTOGRAPH BY MICHAEL KING

Diego Maradona (Argentina), World Cup final,
Azteca Stadium, Mexico City, 1986 (left)

PHOTOGRAPH BY GERARD VANDYSTADT

Peter Beardsley (England), Rous Cup, Wembley, 1988 (above)

PHOTOGRAPH BY BEN RADFORD

Argentina v Bulgaria, World Cup, Mexico, 1986 (right)

PHOTOGRAPH BY BILLY RADFORD

❝I'm gradually acquiring the mentality of an out-and-out defender.
I still like to get forward into attacking positions, but I've had to accept that my role
has changed, and my priorities are now defensive. Having played further forward helps me
as a defender, though. Often I can look in an attacker's eyes and guess how he's going
to take me on. Anticipation is three-quarters of the defender's art.❞

– FERNANDO HIERRO –
REAL MADRID AND SPAIN

**Jimmy Greaves (Tottenham Hotspur) v Burnley,
White Hart Lane, 1963** (above)

**Gordon Banks (Leicester) v Tottenham Hotspur,
FA Cup final, Wembley, 1961** (left)

PHOTOGRAPHS ALLSPORT HISTORICAL COLLECTION © HULTON GETTY

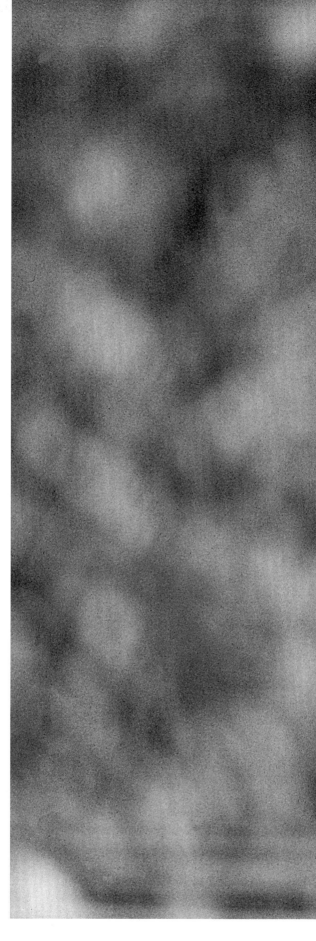

Ryan Giggs and Paul Ince (Manchester United),
Elland Road, Leeds, 1994 (above)

PHOTOGRAPH BY CLIVE BRUNSKILL

David Beckham (Manchester United),
Charity Shield, Wembley, 1996 (right)

PHOTOGRAPH BY SHAUN BOTTERILL

Edwin Van Der Sar (Holland),
European Championships,
Villa Park, 1996 (left)

PHOTOGRAPH BY RICHARD MARTIN

Juninho (Middlesbrough),
Selhurst Park, 1997 (right)

PHOTOGRAPH BY MICHAEL COOPER

Nathan Blake and Per Frandsen
(Bolton), The Hawthorns, 1996
(below right)

PHOTOGRAPH BY GARY M PRIOR

Brazilian fans, World Cup, Mexico, 1986 (above)

Bebeto, World Cup, USA, 1994 (opposite above)

PHOTOGRAPHS BY DAVID CANNON

Claudio Belucci (Sampdoria),
European Cup-Winners' Cup, Genoa, 1995 (opposite left)

PHOTOGRAPH BY GARY M PRIOR

Gheorghe Hagi, (Romania), World Cup, USA, 1994
(opposite centre)

PHOTOGRAPH BY JONATHON DANIELS

David Seaman (Arsenal),
FA Cup semi-final, Wembley, 1993 (opposite right)

PHOTOGRAPH BY SHAUN BOTTERILL

'We played against the Brazilians in 1982 and they are the best team I have ever played against. They were so far in front of any other team it was amazing that they did not go on to win that World Cup in Spain. They played with the attitude that if the opposition scored four then they would score five but only one team has ever managed to do that and that was the Brazilian team of 1970. Playing for Scotland against that Brazilian side in 1982 was an education.

'When you're growing up and you think about the European Cup you think of Real Madrid and I was lucky enough to play against them. When you think about the World Cup you think of Brazil and I was fortunate to play against them also.'

– ALAN HANSEN –

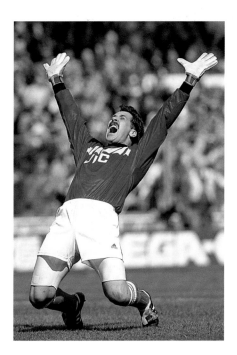

Park football,
London, 1995 (right)

PHOTOGRAPH BY SIMON BRUTY

Beach football,
Dubai, 1991 (below right)

PHOTOGRAPH BY RUSSELL CHEYNE

"For me, Ronaldo is the
complete centre-forward.
Apart from being a goalscorer
of the highest order, he has the
ability to work the ball well
and is a fantastic dribbler.
Most centre-forwards have
an instinct and appetite for goals
but they cannot claim to have
the same ability on the ball."

– JUNINHO –
BRAZIL

**Romario (Brazil)
and Franco Baresi (Italy),
World Cup final,
USA, 1994** (left)

PHOTOGRAPH BY SIMON BRUTY

Jurgen Klinsmann (Bayern Munich), 1996 (above)

PHOTOGRAPH BY BEN RADFORD

Gianluca Vialli (Chelsea), Old Trafford, 1996 (left)

PHOTOGRAPH BY CLIVE BRUNSKILL

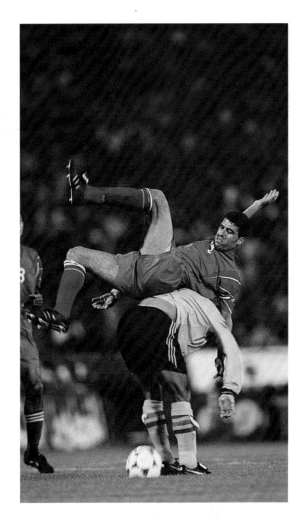

Nouredine Naybet (Morocco) and Kim Tyrone Grant (Ghana),
World Cup qualifyer, Casablanca, 1997

PHOTOGRAPHS BY CLIVE BRUNSKILL

Lee Sharpe (Manchester United) and Darren Beckford (Oldham),
FA Cup semi-final, Wembley, 1994 (above)

PHOTOGRAPH BY CLIVE BRUNSKILL

Andre Kana Biyik (Cameroon) and Carlos Valderrama (Columbia),
World Cup, Italy, 1990 (right)

PHOTOGRAPH BY DAVID CANNON

Stephen Carr (Tottenham Hotspur), Goodison Park, 1997 (above)

PHOTOGRAPH BY GARY M PRIOR

Dave Watson (Everton) and Brian Stein (Luton), Goodison Park, 1987 (left)

PHOTOGRAPH BY SIMON BRUTY

'my philosophy is that when the game starts my work as a manager should be done. The whole process would be first started by having my scout watch my team's opponents. Then, together, we would analyse all the options. My intention was not to be bothered about their strengths, but to find the weakest elements, so we could intensify our pressure on those positions.

'Simply put, the weaker the position, the more we would attack it. I always had the impression that such an approach works better for players. Instead of having them worry about their opponents, I preferred to create a belief that no team was as strong as was said or written.'

– JOHAN CRUYFF –

Alex McLeish (Scotland) and Gary Lineker (England), Rous Cup, Wembley, 1988

PHOTOGRAPH BY SIMON BRUTY

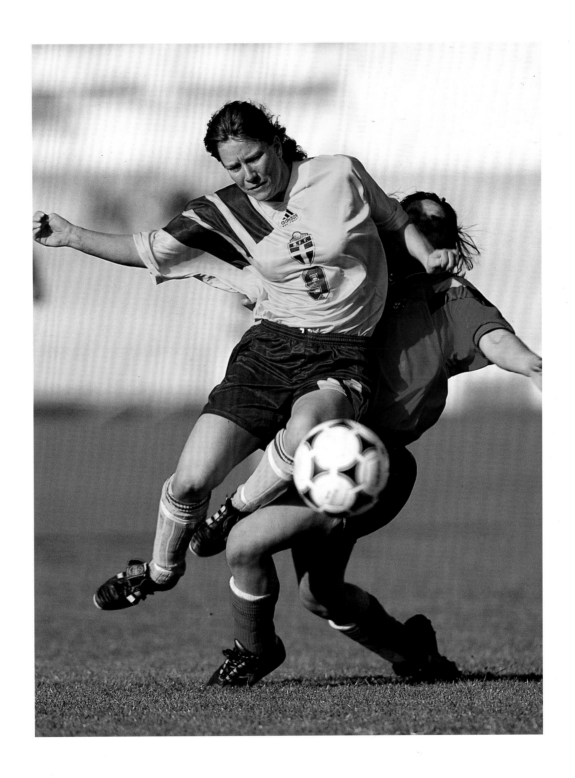

Helen Nilsson (Sweden), Algarve Cup, Portugal, 1994 (above)

PHOTOGRAPH BY SHAUN BOTTERILL

Gary Mabbutt (Tottenham Hotspur) and Kevin Campbell (Arsenal),
Charity Shield, Wembley, 1991 (left)

PHOTOGRAPH BY SIMON BRUTY

Fabio Carannante (Napoli)
and Sergio Batistini (Milan),
San Paolo, 1984

PHOTOGRAPH BY DAVID CANNON

Daniel Prodan (Romania),
World Cup, USA, 1994 (above)

PHOTOGRAPH BY SHAUN BOTTERILL

Roberto Baggio misses a penalty,
Brazil v Italy, World Cup final,
USA, 1994 (left)

PHOTOGRAPH BY MIKE POWELL

⌈Nobody can do it for you. When I step up to take a penalty, there's no pressman or fan to help me with it. I have to do it, and if I fail, it's my responsibility. So I get on with it. It's my job and I know I'm willing to take the flak if I fail. That's how I play. I take responsibility.⌋

– STUART PEARCE –
NOTTINGHAM FOREST AND ENGLAND

Paul Gascoigne (England), World Cup, Italy, 1990 (above)
PHOTOGRAPH BY BILLY STICKLAND

Stuart Pearce (England), European Championships, Wembley, 1996 (left)
PHOTOGRAPH BY BEN RADFORD

Salvatore Schillaci (Italy), World Cup, Italy, 1990 (above left)

PHOTOGRAPH BY SIMON BRUTY

Enrico Chiesa (Italy), European Championships, Anfield, 1996 (above right)

PHOTOGRAPH BY SHAUN BOTTERILL

Luis Enrique (Spain), World Cup, USA, 1994 (left)

PHOTOGRAPH BY SIMON BRUTY

Nigel Spink (Aston Villa), Villa Park, 1992 (above)

PHOTOGRAPH BY BEN RADFORD

Pierluigi Casiraghi and Gianfranco Zola,
Italy v Russia, European Championships, Anfield, 1996, (left)

PHOTOGRAPH BY MIKE HEWITT

Janne Rasmussen (Denmark)
Algarve Cup, 1994 (right)
PHOTOGRAPH BY SHAUN BOTTERILL

Paul Merson (Arsenal),
FA Cup semi-final, Wembley,
1993 (below)
PHOTOGRAPH BY SHAUN BOTTERILL

Marco Tardelli (Italy),
World Cup final, Madrid, 1982
(far right)
PHOTOGRAPH BY ALLSPORT

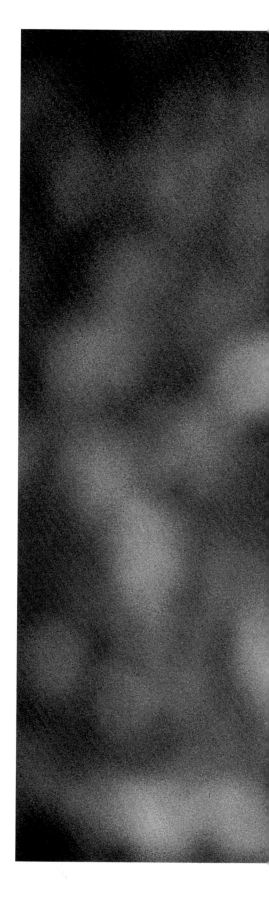

the final whistle

‘The most memorable celebrations I experienced after a match were on winning three League championships with Barcelona. Three times we became champions on the last day. On each occasion we were completely dependent on the results of our rivals. But twice Real Madrid lost at Tenerife and once Deportivo La Coruna couldn't win at home to Valencia.

'The last one was especially exciting because with the score at 0-0 La Coruna missed a penalty in the 90th minute. I'll never forget the tension in the Nou Camp on and off the pitch when players and fans had to wait a couple of minutes for the result of a game elsewhere in Spain. And then that enormous burst of joy, when everyone found out that we had indeed won in the closest finish possible.'

– JOHAN CRUYFF –

World Cup final, Spain, 1982 (above)
PHOTOGRAPH BY STEVE POWELL

World Cup final, Wembley, 1966 (right)
PHOTOGRAPH ALLSPORT HISTORICAL COLLECTION © HULTON GETTY

Ruud Gullit and Gerald Vanenberg,
European Championships, Olympic Stadium, Munich, 1988
("the final whistle", pages 172-173)
PHOTOGRAPH BY BILLY STICKLAND

Portsmouth fans, FA Cup quarter-final v Chelsea, Fratton Park, 1997

PHOTOGRAPH BY PHIL COLE

Roker Park, 1997 (above right)
PHOTOGRAPH BY MARK THOMPSON

David Ginola (Newcastle)
with ball boy, St James' Park,
1996 (right)
PHOTOGRAPH BY STU FORSTER

Pele (Brazil) and Bobby Moore
(England), World Cup, Mexico,
1970 (far right)
PHOTOGRAPH ALLSPORT HISTORICAL
COLLECTION © MSI

Schoolboy football, 1932 (above)

Bobby Moore (England), World Cup final, Wembley, 1966 (left)

Alessandro Del Piero (Juventus), 1997 (above)
PHOTOGRAPH BY CLIVE MASON

Jack Charlton (Eire manager), Eire v England, Dublin, 1995 (right)
PHOTOGRAPH BY BILLY STICKLAND

Fernando Caceres
(Real Zaragoza)
European Cup-Winners'
Cup final, Paris, 1995 (left)
PHOTOGRAPH BY RICHARD MARTIN

Neil Tovey (South Africa)
and Nelson Mandela,
African Nations Cup final,
South Africa, 1996 (above right)
PHOTOGRAPH BY MARK THOMPSON

Hudspith (Newcastle),
FA Cup final, Wembley, 1924
(below right)
PHOTOGRAPH ALLSPORT HISTORICAL
COLLECTION © HULTON GETTY

'**a**fter a game we would have a bath then, if it was a home game, I would go and meet my wife in the players' lounge. We'd have a couple of drinks then, if my dad had come down from Scotland to watch the game, we'd go and have a drink with him. Then my wife and myself would go and have a meal.

'If we had lost I would still go out but I would be enjoying it a lot less than if we had won. If you had got beaten playing for Liverpool you wouldn't recover until the next game you played. The psychological difference between winning and losing is quite incredible. I think the biggest thing about football now is you get three points for a win, one for a draw and none for a defeat. That may sound as if I'm stating the obvious but it has had a big effect. Psychologically, the difference between winning and drawing is not that much. But I can't begin to tell you the difference between winning and losing! If you got beaten the psychological feeling of getting beaten is a nightmare!

'There's so much tension beforehand that if you have won then there's a great feeling of satisfaction that leads to laughing and joking. If you get beaten then you have got pressure throughout the next week.'

– ALAN HANSEN –

Harry Johnston and Stanley Matthews (Blackpool), FA Cup final, Wembley, 1953 (above)
PHOTOGRAPH ALLSPORT HISTORICAL COLLECTION © HULTON GETTY

Jurgen Kohler (West Germany), World Cup final, Italy, 1990 (left)
PHOTOGRAPH BY SIMON BRUTY

'I think the most frenetic atmosphere I can remember at any game was at the 1986 Cup final. We were playing against Everton and had pipped Everton for the championship so, as well as it being a Merseyside derby, we were going for the double. The Everton and Liverpool fans were desegregated so Wembley was a sea of red and blue.

'We won 3-1 and the next day the two teams went round Liverpool. We were in an open-topped bus with the cup and the Everton players were in another bus a couple of hundred yards behind us – I don't know how they were feeling but I'm glad it was them and not us.'

– ALAN HANSEN –

George Best, with girlfriend Jennifer Lowe
(Miss UK), 1966 (above)

Photograph Allsport Historical Collection © MSI

Wimbledon FA Cup victory parade, 1988 (left)

Photograph by Pascal Rondeau

'On the second occasion we won the title in my time at Liverpool I was waiting in the dressing-room expecting us to start on a lap of honour. Then Ronnie Moran came in holding a box in his hand and said, "Who's played 13 games?" You had to have played a minimum of 13 League games to be entitled to receive a championship medal. He then took the medals out of the box and threw them at everyone who was due to receive one. Then he said, "We've had a great season. Enjoy the next week but no longer. It'll be even tougher to win it next year."

'I'd been expecting to be on a lap of honour for six months, especially as in that season, 1978-79, our record had been a bit special. Over 42 games, we had scored 85 goals and let 16 in and that's a record that I don't think will ever be beaten.'

ALAN HANSEN

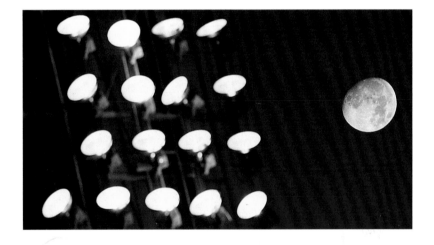

Hillsborough tributes, Anfield, 1989 (left)

PHOTOGRAPH BY PASCAL RONDEAU

Amsterdam Arena, 1997 (above right)
PHOTOGRAPH BY SHAUN BOTTERILL

Floodlights, RFK Stadium, Washington, World Cup, 1994 (centre right)
PHOTOGRAPH BY BILLY STICKLAND

View from St James' Park, 1996 (below right)
PHOTOGRAPH BY ANTON WANT

'**a**fter a match I would wind down mentally more or less immediately. To get the stress out of my body would take longer. That's why I would always go home soon after the match. Far away from the stress and the hectic atmosphere at the stadium your body relaxes better and faster.'

– JOHAN CRUYFF –

Wembley, 1994 (right)

PHOTOGRAPH BY CLIVE MASON

Visions of Football

The photographs in this book have been selected from the
extensive football library of Allsport, the world's leading sports picture agency.
The photographs and their availability in all corners of the world
would not have been possible without the help of the following:
The Photographers, Picture Researchers, Darkroom Staff,
Picture Desk Operators, Accounts Staff, Clerical Staff
and everyone else in the Allsport offices at

ALLSPORT UK
3 Greenlea Park
Prince George's Road
London SW19 2JD

Tel: (0181) 685 1010 • Fax: (0181) 648 5240

ALLSPORT USA
Allsport Building,
17383 Sunset Boulevard,
Pacific Palisades,
California 90272-4191

Tel: (310) 230 3400 • Fax: (310) 573 7600

ALLSPORT NEW YORK
13B Gramercy Place
280 Park Avenue South
New York 10010

Tel: (212) 979 0903 • Fax: (212) 979 0460

and the international network of agencies
on all five continents.

ALLSPORT WEBSITE
http://www.allsport.com

SOURCES OF QUOTES

Shearer: Scotland on Sunday, 1997; Puskas: The International Football Book Number 3, 1961 (Souvenir Press Ltd, edited by Stratton Smith);
Pearce: The Sunday Times, 1996; Maldini: World Soccer, 1997; Platini: video, Platini, Soccer Superstar, 1988;
Hierro: World Soccer, 1997; Collins: Scotland on Sunday, 1996; Johnstone: interview with Graham McColl, 1995;
Juninho: Total Sport, 1997; Henry: World Soccer, 1997; Lambert: Scotland on Sunday, 1996;
Gullit: Prospect, 1997; Best: Inside Football, 1990; Dalglish: The Herald, 1997

ANDRE
DEUTSCH